Impressum
Verlag: BABADADA GmbH, Nedderfeld 112 , 22529 Hamburg
Geschäftsführer / Verlagsleitung: Harald Hof
Druck: Books on Demand GmbH, In de Tarpen 42, 22848 Norderstedt

Imprint
Publisher: BABADADA GmbH, Nedderfeld 112 , 22529 Hamburg, Germany
Managing Director / Publishing direction: Harald Hof
Print: Books on Demand GmbH, In de Tarpen 42, 22848 Norderstedt

classroom
siklyovimasko than

divide
ulavibe vordon

186/2

board
tabla

school yard
školaki avlin

teacher
sikavno

paper
lil

write
hramovibe

pen
kalemi tintasa

desk
masa butyake

ruler
lenyiri

book
lil

pupil
siklo

satchel
dumeski tašna

pencil case
kalemengi kutia

pencil
kalemi

pencil sharpener
kalemengi čhurori

rubber
kosimaski guma

drawing pad
čitrimasko bloko

drawing

čitribe

paintbrush

boyimaski frča

paint box

boyimaski kutia

scissors

kata

glue

lepako

exercise book

bukjardarimasko lil

homework

khereski buti

number

gendo

add

džide

subtract

ikal

multiply

multiplicirin

calculate

kalkulirin

letter

hramome lil

alphabet

alfabeta

word

lafo

text

teksti

read

drabaribe

chalk

kreda

lesson

lekciya

register

Klasesko registro

examination

egzameni

certificate

sertifikato

school uniform

školaki uniforma

education

edukacia

encyclopedia

enciklopedia

university

univerziteto

microscope

mikroskopo

map

mapa

waste-paper basket

korpa čhudimaske lila

hotel
hoteli

Grand

hostel
Lačhi blevel!

currency exchange office
biro baši devize

suitcase
koferi

car
vordon

language

ćhib

yes / no

va / na

Okay

Okay

hello

Namaste

translator

tumači

Thank you

Ov sasto

how much is…?

Kozom si…?

I don´t get it

Na havava

problem

problemo

Good evening!

Lačhi rat!

Good morning!

Lačhi javin!

Good night!

Lačhi rat!

goodbye

ačhon Devlesa

direction

dromeski sikavin

luggage

bagaži

bag

gono

backpack

dumesko gono

guest

misafiri

room

kamara

sleeping bag

sovimasko gono

tent

cerha

tourist information

turistikani informacia

beach

plaža

credit card

kreditno kartica

breakfast

javinako habe

lunch

kušluko

dinner

ratyako habe

Ticket

karta

elevator

elevatori

stamp

marka

border

simantra

customs

adetia

embassy

ambasada

visa

viza

passport

pašaporti

airplane
avioni

ship
baro vapori

fire truck
jagako motori

bus
autobusi

truck
kamionia

motorboat
vapori ko motori

car
vordon

bike
biciklo

ferry

feri vapori

boat

vapori

motorbike

motorciklo

police car

policiako vordon

racing car

prastamasko vordon

rental car

rentakar

car sharing

ulavibe vordon

tow truck

rumosardo kamioni

garbage truck

kamionengo than

engine

motori

fuel

petroli

fuel station

petrolesko stasioni

traffic sign

trafikoskere išaretia

traffic

trafiko

traffic jam

baro trafiko

parking lot

vordonesko parkirimasko than

train station

pampurengo stasioni

tracks

kamionia

train

pampuri

tram

tramvaj

wagon

vagoni

helicopter

helikopteri

airport

aeroporti

tower

kula

passenger

dromarutno

container

kontejneri

carton

kartoni

cart

vordonoro

basket

sevli

take off / land

urjalipasko starto /
urjalipasko agor

city

diz

village

gav

city center

dizyako centro

house

kher

movie theater
sinema

advert
avazikerutni

street light
dromeski lamba

street
drom

taxi
taksisti

snack shop
kiosk

pedestrian
nakhimasko than

sidewalk
trotoari

zebra crossing
zebra nakhimaski

dumpster
gunoengi bari kanta

crossing
nakhimasko than

traffic lights
semafori

hut
koliba

apartment
apartmani

train station
pampurengo stasioni

city hall
dizyaki sala

museum
muzeji

school
škola

university

univerziteto

bank

banka

hospital

hospitalo

hotel

hoteli

pharmacy

apoteka

office

ofiso

book shop

lil bikinimasko than

shop

dukyano

flower shop

lulugengo bikinutno

supermarket

supermarket

market

kurko

department store

baro bikinimasko kher

fishmonger's shop

mačhengo astarutno

mall

kinimasko centro

harbor

vaporengo ačhovimasko than

park

parko

bench

klupa

bridge

purt

stairs

merdevenya

subway

metro stasioni

tunnel

tuneli

bus stop

autobuseski adžikerin

bar

bar

restaurant

restorani

postbox

poštako mohto

street sign

dromesko išareti

parking meter

parking than

zoo

zoo

swimming pool

nangyovimasko bazeni

mosque

džamiya

farm
farma

pollution
melalipe

cemetery
limorengo than

church
khangeri

playground
khelimasko than

temple
hramo

landscape
pejzaži

leaf
patrin

signpost
išareti

path
drom

meadow
livazin

stone
bar

tree
kašt

hiker
phiravno

river
len

grass
čar

flower
luludi

valley

harno than

hill

bairi

lake

devrijal

forest

veš

desert

mulano than

volcano

vulkano

castle

saraji

rainbow

renkali badalin

mushroom

gaba

palm tree

palma kašt

mosquito

sivrija

fly

mak

ant

karandža

bee

birumni

spider

pauko

landscape - pejzaži

15

beetle

buba

frog

žamba

squirrel

ververica

hedgehog

kanzauri

hare

šošoj

owl

buf

bird

pakšin

swan

lebedi

boar

bali

deer

eleno

moose

eleno

dam

pani garavin

wind turbine

bavlalaki turbina

solar panel

solarno paneli

climate

klima

waiter
kelneri

menu
menije

chair
sandaliya

soup
čorba

pizza
pica

cutlery
habasko alati

tablecloth
poftaneski salfetka

starter
avgo habe

main course
šerutno habe

dessert
gudlimata

drinks
piiba

food
habe

bottle
šiša

fast food

fast food

street food

sokakongo habe

teapot

čajniko

sugar bowl

šekereskoro čaroro

portion

porcia

espresso machine

makina vaš espresso

high chair

uči sandaliya

bill

esapi

tray

apladiya

knife

čhuri

fork

vilyuška

spoon

roj

teaspoon

čajeski roj

serviette

salfetka

glass

tahtai

plate

čaro

soup plate

čaro čorbake

saucer

hor čaro

sauce

sosi

salt shaker

londesko čaroro

pepper mill

kale biberesko pišlo

vinegar

šut

oil

zejtini

spices

začinia

ketchup

kečap

mustard

senf

mayonnaise

majonezi

special offer
specialno oferta

customer
mušteriya

FOR

dairy products
thudeske butya

fruit
emiši

shopping cart
vordonoro

butcher's shop
kasapi

bakery
furuna

weigh
ladavipe

vegetables
zarzavati

meat
masesko rolati

frozen food
pahome habe

cold cuts

šudro mas

canned food

konzerva

detergent

thovimasko prašako

candy

gudlimata

household products

khereske butya

cleaning products

užarimaske butya

sales representative

bikinutno

cash register

kasapi

cashier

kasieri

shopping list

kinimaski patrin

opening hours

putarimaske satura

wallet

lovengi tašna

credit card

kreditno kartica

bag

gono

plastic bag

plastikano gono

water

pani

juice

džus

milk

thud

coke

kola

wine

mol

beer

bira

alcohol

alkohol

cocoa

kakao

tea

čaj

coffee

kafa

espresso

espresso

cappuccino

cappuccino

banana

banana

apple

phabaj

orange

portokali

melon

kavuni

lemon

limoni

carrot

karota

garlic

sir

bamboo

bambusi

onion

purum

mushroom

gaba

nuts

akhora

noodles

humereske butya

spaghetti

špageti

rice

rezo

salad

salata

fries

čipsi

fried potatoes

peke kompiria

pizza

pica

hamburger

hamburger

sandwich

sendviči

escalope

kotleti

ham

žamboni

salami

salama

sausage

goja

chicken

khajnako mas

roast

peko

fish

mačho

food - habe

porridge oats

popara

muesli

musli

cornflakes

kornfleks

flour

varo

croissant

kroasani

bread roll

masesko rolati

bread

maro

toast

tosti

cookies

biskotia

butter

puteri

curd

urda

cake

torta

egg

jaro

fried egg

peke jare

cheese

kiral

ice cream

šudro gudlo

sugar

šekeri

honey

avgin

jelly

džem

nougat cream

čokoladaki krema

curry

kari

farm house
farmako kher

straw bale
bale pus

barn
hasari

field
umal

horse
grast

trailer
indžarimasko vordon

tractor
traktori

foal
grastoro

donkey
her

sheep
bakhroro

lamb
bakhroro

goat

buzno

cow

guruvni

calf

guruvoro

pig

balo

piglet

baloro

bull

guruv

goose

papin

duck

payka

chick

pilička

hen

khayni

cockerel

bašno

rat

baro germuso

cat

bilika

mouse

germuso

ox

guruv

dog

džukel

dog house

džukelesko kher

garden hose

žardina

watering can

panyarimaski kanta

scythe

aindžako kidimasko alati

plow

plugo

sickle

srpo

hoe

motika

pitchfork

aindžaki vilyuška

axe

tover

pushcart

vordonoro phiravutno

trough

balani

milk can

thudeski šiša

sack

harari

fence

trujalutni

stable

jahri

greenhouse

haryalo kher

soil

phuv

seed

seme

fertilizer

gyubre

combine harvester

aindžako kidipe

harvest

kidibe aindž

harvest

harmani

yams

phuvaki phabaj

wheat

giv

soya

soja

potato

kompiri

corn

mumuruzi

rapeseed

šarlagani

fruit tree

emišengo kašt

manioc

Kasava

grain

giveskere javinlukoja

chimney
odžako

roof
učharin khereski

downspout
cevka

window
pendžarka

garage
garaža

doorbell
udaresko zili

door
udar

trash can
gunoeski korpa

mailbox
mohto

garden
bavča

living room
bešimaski kamara

bathroom
banya

kitchen
kujna

bedroom
sovimasko than

kids room
čhavengi kamara

dining room
than hajbaske rakjako habe

floor

kati

wall

duvari

ceiling

tavano

cellar

špajzi

sauna

sauna

balcony

terasa

terrace

terasa

pool

bazeni

lawn mower

čar harnyarimaski makina

sheet

patrin

bedspread

čaršafia

bed

kreveto

broom

šulavni

bucket

korpa

switch

elektrikani phabarin

wallpaper
tapeta

picture
tasviri

lamp
lamba

shelf
rafti

cabinet
ormari

television
televiziya

fireplace
jagako than

flower
luludi

cushion
šerand

vase
vazna

sofa
sofa

remote control
durutni komanda

carpet

kilimi

drape

perde

table

masa

chair

sandaliya

rocking chair

kunajka sandaliya

armchair

fotelya

book

lil

blanket

kebe

decoration

dekoraciya

firewood

kašta phabarimaske

film

filmi

stereo system

stereo ašunimaske butya

key

nahtari

newspaper

gazeta

painting

frčaja bojakeribe

poster

posteri

radio

radio

notebook

hramovimasko bloko

vacuum cleaner

elektrikani šulavni

cactus

kaktusi

candle

momoli

fridge
frižideri

microwave oven
mikrodalgaki rerna

kitchen scales
kujnako kantari

toaster
tosteri

laundry detergent
detergenti

freezer
hor pahonimaski komora

stove
furna

trash can
gunoeski korpa

dishwasher
detergenti čarenge

cooker
....
keravimasko than

pot
....
čaro

cast-iron pot
....
sastrnali tendžera

wok / kadai
....
vok cihani

pan
....
tava

kettle
....
elektrikano bokali

steamer

tendžera ki para

baking tray

tepsija

crockery

čare

mug

bareder fildžano

bowl

čaro

chopsticks

kinakere habaskere kaštore

ladle

fioka

spatula

špatula

whisk

vastesko mikseri

strainer

cedimasko čaro

sieve

porizen

grater

rende

mortar

avano

barbecue

skara

fireplace

puteribe jag

chopping board

čhinimaski tabla

rolling pin

oklagia

corkscrew

puterimasko alati

can

konzerva

can opener

konzervako puterutno

oven cloth

čaresko ikerutno

sink

lavabo

brush

frča

sponge

sungeri

blender

mikseri

deep freezer

hor pahonimasko frižideri

baby bottle

bebeski šiša

tap

češma

heating
tataripe

shower
tuširibe

towel
peškiri

shower curtain
tuširimaski perda

bubble bath
nanyovibe sapuneske balonencar

bathtub
kada nanyovimaske

glass
tahtai

washing machine
makina thovimaske šeja

tap
češma

tiles
pločke

potty
turako

sink
lavabo

toilet	squat toilet	bidet
toaleti	toaleti bešimasa ko pundre	bide

urinal	toilet paper	toilet brush
pisoari	toaletesko lil	frča toalateske

toothbrush

danda thovimaski frča

toothpaste

danda thovimaski krema

dental floss

dandesko thav

wash

thovibe danda

hand shower

vasteskoro tuši

douche

tuši

basin

lavabo

back brush

dumeski frča

soap

sapuni

shower gel

tuširimasko geli

shampoo

šamponi

flannel

flanela

drain

kada ćidimaske pani

creme

krema

deodorant

dezodoransi

mirror

ajna

hand mirror

vasteski ajna

razor

žileti moravimaske

shaving foam

moravimaski pena

aftershave

palal muravimaski krema

comb

kanglik

brush

frča

hair-dryer

feni balenge

hairspray

sprej balenge

makeup

šminka

lipstick

karmini

nail varnish

oja najenge

cotton wool

pamuko pošom

nail scissors

kata najenge

perfume

parfemi

washbag

gono thovimaske

stool

sandaliya

weighing scales

tereziya

bathrobe

bademantili

rubber gloves

gumena kalcunya

tampon

tamponi

sanitary towel

toaletno lil

chemical toilet

hemikano toaleti

alarm clock
alarmesko sato

cuddly toy
mangli khelutni

toy car
vordonora khelimaske

rattle
tropalka

doll's house
bebedžikongo kher

present
bakšiši

balloon

baloni

bed

kreveto

stroller

bebengo vordon

deck of cards

špili karte

jigsaw

ker-rumin khelin

comic

komikano lil

lego bricks

lego kocke

toy blocks

kocke khelimaske

action figure

akciaki figura

romper suit

bodi bebeske

frisbee

frizbi

mobile

mobile

board game

masa khelimaske

dice

zari

model train set

pampuri khelimaske

pacifier

cucla

party

bahlana

picture book

tasvirengo lil

ball

topka

doll

bebedžiko

play

khelibe

sandpit

pošikako than

swing

kuna

toys

khelimaske butya

video game console

konzola video khelimaske

tricycle

triciklo

teddy bear

poftaneski ričini

wardrobe

garderoba

clothing
šeja

socks

kalcunya

stockings

khuvde kalcunya

tights

hulahopke

scarf
momija

umbrella
čadori

t-shirt
maica

belt
kaiši

boots
čizme

slippers
papuče

sneakers
trenerke

sandals

sandale

shoes

menije

rubber boots

gumena čizme

underwear

sostenya

bra

eleko

undershirt

jeleko

clothing - šeja

body
bodi

pants
pantalonya

jeans
farmerke

skirt
suknya

blouse
bluza

shirt
gat

pullover
puloveri

sweater
dukseri

blazer
harno kaputi

jacket
džeketi

coat
kaputi

raincoat
biršimdesko mantili

costume
kostimi

dress
fustano

wedding dress
prandinako fustano

suit

kostumi

nightgown

rakjako fustano

pajamas

pižame

sari

sari

headscarf

momija šereske

turban

turbani

burka

burka

kaftan

kaftani

abaya

abaya

swimsuit

nangyovimaske šeja

trunks

buxle pantolonya

shorts

harne pantolonya

tracksuit

sporteske trenerke

apron

kecelya

gloves

vasteske kalcunya

button

kopča

glasses

gjuzlukya

bracelet

belegziya

necklace

mirikle

ring

angrustik

earring

čeni

cap

stadik

coat hanger

kaputeski čiviya

hat

stadik

tie

kravata

zip

patenti

helmet

kaciga

braces

dandenge proteze

school uniform

školaki uniforma

uniform

uniforma

bib

ligarka

pacifier

cucla

diaper

pherno

office

ofiso

server
serveri

filing cabinet
raftija dokumentenca

printer
printeri

monitor
monitori

paper
lil

desk
masa butyake

mouse
mausi

folder
folderi

keyboard
tastatura

waste-paper basket
korpa čhudimaske lila

chair
sandaliya

computer
kompjuteri

coffee mug

fildžano kafake

calculator

kalkulatori

internet

internet

laptop

laptop

letter

lil

message

mesaži

cell phone

mobilno telefono

network

netvorko

photocopier

kopirimaski makina

software

softveri

telephone

telefono

plug socket

štekeri

fax machine

faks makina

form

formulari

document

dokumento

buy

kinibe

pay

pokinibe

trade

kino-bikinibe

money

love

dollar

dolari

euro

euro

yen

jeni

rouble

rublya

Swiss franc

švajcariako franko

renminbi yuan

renminbi juan

rupee

rupija

cash point

lovengo automati

currency exchange office

biro baši devize

gold

somnakaj

silver

rup

oil

petroli

energy

energia

price

fiyati

contract

kontrakto

tax

taksa

stock

berzaki akcija

work

butikeribe

employee

butyarno

employer

butyako dendutno

factory

fabrika

shop

dukyano

economy - ekonomia

police officer
Policiako oficero

fireman
jagako aćhavutno

cook
habekerutno

doctor
doktoro

pilot
piloti

gardener
bavčako butyarno

carpenter
tišleri

seamstress
šnajderka

judge
krisuno

chemist
hemičari

actor
akteri

bus driver

autobusesko šoferi

taxi driver

taksisti

fisherman

mačhengo astarutno

cleaning lady

užarutni

roofer

učharinengo kerutno

waiter

kelneri

hunter

avdžija

painter

tasvirkerutno

baker

furnadžia

electrician

elektrikako phirno

builder

tamirutno

engineer

inžinjeri

butcher

kasapi

plumber

panjesko butyarno

postman

poštari

occupations - profesie

soldier

askeri

architect

arhitekto

cashier

kasieri

florist

luludyari

hairdresser

frizeri

conductor

kondukteri

mechanic

mekanisti

captain

kapetani

dentist

dandengo saslyarno

scientist

vigjanalo manuš

rabbi

rabini

imam

imami

monk

rašaj

pastor

rašaj

hammer
čekiči

pliers
silavja

screwdriver
šrafcigeri

wrench
mekanikane nahtaria

torch
fakeli

excavator
hrandimasko alati

toolbox
alateski kutia

ladder
merdeveni

saw
pila

nails
karfa

drill
posavin

repair

lačharkeribe

shovel

lopata

Damn!

Naleti!

dustpan

vatrali

paint can

lonco bojimaske

screws

šrafja

musical instruments
muzikane instrumentia

loud speaker
bare avazesko šunutno

drum set
davulenge butya

guitar
gitara

double bass
duplo bas

trumpet
truba

piano

piano

violin

kemana

bass

bas

timpani

timpani

drums

davulia

keyboard

sintisajzeri

saxophone

saksafoni

flute

flejta

microphone

mikrofoni

musical instruments - muzikane instrumentia

entrance
khuvin

tiger
tigari

cage
kafezi

zebra
zebra nakhimaski

animal feed
hajvanengo parvaripe

panda
panda

animals
hajvania

elephant
elefanti

kangaroo
kenguri

rhino
rino

gorilla
gorila

bear
ričini

camel

kamila

ostrich

ostriga

lion

aslani

monkey

majmuni

flamingo

flamingo

parrot

papagali

polar bear

polarno ričini

penguin

pingvini

shark

ajkula

peacock

pauno

snake

sap

crocodile

krokodilo

zookeeper

zoo arakhutno

seal

foka

jaguar

jaguari

pony

poni

leopard

leopardi

hippo

hipo

giraffe

žirafa

eagle

zorale kandžengi paškin

boar

bali

fish

mačho

turtle

želka

walrus

morži

fox

lumri

gazelle

gazela

sports
sportia

American football
Amerikako fudbali

cycling
biciklizmo

tennis
tenis

basketball
basketboli

swimming
nangjovibe

boxing
boksi

ice hockey
hokej ko paho

soccer
fudbali

badminton
badmington

athletics
atletika

handball
vasteskoboli

skiing
skiibe

polo
polo

laugh
asaibe

jump
hutibe

hug
deibe angali

walk
phiribe

sing
giljavibe

dream
dikhibe suno

pray
azirikeribe

kiss
čumibe

write

hramovibe

draw

čitribe

show

sikavibe

push

cidljaribe

give

deibe

take

leibe

have

isibe

do

keribe

be

te ovel

stand

tergyovibe

run

prastaibe

pull

cidibe

throw

čhudibe

fall

peribe

lie

hovavibe

wait

adžikeribe

carry

phiravibe

sit

bešibe

get dressed

urjavibe

sleep

sovibe

wake up

džangavibe

activities - aktivitetia

look at

dikhibe ko

cry

rovibe

stroke

čalavibe

comb

uhlavibr

talk

vakeribe

understand

haljovibe

ask

puč

listen

šunibe

drink

piibe

eat

habe

tidy up

užaribe

love

kamibe

cook

keribe habe

drive

paldibe vordon

fly

urjalibe

activities - aktivitetia

sail

vaporea džaibe

calculate

kalkulirin

read

drabaribe

learn

sikljovibe

work

butikeribe

marry

prandibe

sew

suvibe

brush teeth

thovibe danda

kill

mudaribe

smoke

piibe dahani

send

bičhalibe

grandmother
mami

grandfather
papu

father
dat

mother
daj

baby
bebe

daughter
čhaj

son
čhavo

guest

misafiri

aunt

bibi

uncle

kako

brother

phral

sister

phen

forehead
čekat

eye
jakh

shoulder
piko

finger
naj

face
muj

chin
vilica

hand
vast

breast
čuči

leg
pundro

arm
musik

baby

bebe

man

murš

woman

džuvli

girl

čhaj

boy

ćhavo

head

šero

back

dumo

belly

maškar

navel

pupko

toe

pundrenge naja

heel

patum

bone

kokalo

hip

kuko

knee

koč

elbow

lahci

nose

nakh

buttocks

bul

skin

mortik

cheek

čham

ear

kan

lip

voš

body - trupo

mouth

muj

tooth

danda

tongue

ćhib

brain

godi

heart

vilo

muscle

muskulo

lung

kolin

liver

buko

stomach

vogi

kidneys

bubrekora

sex

seks

condom

kondomi

ovum

yarengi kletka

semen

sperma

pregnancy

khamnipe

menstruation

menstruaciya

vagina

vagina

penis

penis

eyebrow

phov

hair

bala

neck

men

hospital
hospitalo

ambulance
medicinako vordon

wheelchair
invalidsko vordon

fracture
phagipe

doctor

doktoro

emergency room

sigyarimaski kamara

nurse

medicinaki phen

emergency

sigyaripen

unconscious

ki koma

pain

dukh

injury

dukhavipen

bleeding

ratvaripe

heart attack

infrakto

stroke

šlog

allergy

alergiya

cough

khuinibe

fever

tinanipe

flu

gripa

diarrhea

diyarea

headache

šereski dukh

cancer

kanceri

diabetes

diyabetes

surgeon

operaciya

scalpel

skalperi

operation

operaciya

CT

CT

x-ray

rentgen

ultrasound

ultra avazo

face mask

mujeski maska

disease

nasvalipe

waiting room

adžukyarimasko than

crutch

paterica

plaster

flastero

bandage

phandimaski gaza

injection

inyekciya

stethoscope

stetoskopo

stretcher

tregero

clinical thermometer

klinicko termometro

birth

biyanipe

overweight

baro thulipe

hearing aid

ašunimasko aparato

disinfectant

dezinfekciako

infection

infekciya

virus

viruso

HIV / AIDS

HIV / SIDA

medicine

medicina

vaccination

vakcinaciya

tablets

tabletura

pill

hapi

emergency call

sigyarimasko akharipe

blood pressure monitor

monitori vaš učo pretisak

ill / healthy

nasvalo / sasto

Help!	alarm	assault
Mažutisar!	alarmo	atako

attack	danger	emergency exit
atako	dar buti	sigyarimasko iklyovipen

Fire!	fire extinguisher	accident
Bari jag!	mamuj jagako aparati	bibax

first-aid kit	SOS	police
butya avgo ažutimaske	SOS	Policia

Europe

Evropa

North America

Utarali Amerika

South America

Purabali Amerika

Africa

Afrika

Asia

Azija

Australia

Australia

Atlantic

Atlantiko

Pacific

Pacifiko

Indian Ocean

Indiako Okeano

Antarctic Ocean

Antarktikosko Okeano

Arctic Ocean

Arktikosko Okeano

North pole

Utaralo poli

South pole

Purabalo poli

Antarctica

Antarktiko

earth

phuv

land

phuv

sea

samudra

island

džaziri

nation

nacija

state

raštra

clock face

saatosko gendo

hour hand

saatoski sikavni

minute hand

dakikongi sikavni

second hand

sekundarno saatoski sikavin

What time is it?

Kozom si o saato?

day

dive

time

vrama

now

akana

digital watch

digitalno saato

minute

dakika

hour

časo

Monday
Lujin

Wednesday
trintodi

Friday
Paraskin

Saturday
Savato

Tuesday
Dujtodi

Thursday
Štartodi

Sunday
Purano kurko

yesterday

erati

today

avdive

tomorrow

tajsa

morning

javin

noon

ekvaš dive

evening

blevel

MO	TU	WE	TH	FR	SA	SU
1	2	3	4	5	6	7
8	9	10	11	12	13	14
15	16	17	18	19	20	21
22	23	24	25	26	27	28
29	30	31	1	2	3	4

workdays

butyarne divesa

MO	TU	WE	TH	FR	SA	SU
1	2	3	4	5	6	7
8	9	10	11	12	13	14
15	16	17	18	19	20	21
22	23	24	25	26	27	28
29	30	31	1	2	3	4

weekend

vikend

rain
biršim

rainbow
renkali badalin

snow
iv

wind
bavlal

spring
anglonilaj

fall
palonilaj

summer
nilaj

winter
ivend

4.APRIL	11°	☀
5.APRIL	4°	☁
6.APRIL	13°	☂
7.APRIL	8°	☀
8.APRIL	10°	☀

weather forecast

vramakoro vakeribe

thermometer

termometro

sunshine

khamalo

cloud

badal

fog

muhi

humidity

nemlime hava

lightning

šemšekoja

thunder

šemšekosko čalavibe

storm

bura

hail

kijameti

monsoon

monsuni

flood

baro pani

ice

paho

January

Januaro

February

Februaro

March

Marto

April

Aprilo

May

Majo

June

Juno

July

Julo

August

Augusto

September

Septembro

October

Oktombro

November

Novembro

December

Dekembro

shapes
forme

circle

rota

square

kvadrati

rectangle

rektanglo

triangle

trianglo

sphere

sfera

cube

kocka

colors
boje

white
parni

yellow
galbeno

orange
pomarandža

pink
roze

red
loli

purple
lila

blue
vunato

green
harjali

brown
kafeno

gray
kuršumlija

black
kali

a lot / a little

but / hari

angry / calm

holjame / mudro

beautiful / ugly

šuži / bišuži

beginning / end

starto / agor

big / small

baro / tikno

bright / dark

puterde bojako / phanle
bojako

brother / sister

phral / phen

clean / dirty

užo / melalo

complete / incomplete

sahno / bisahno

day / night

dive / rat

dead / alive

mulo / dživdo

wide / narrow

buvlo / tank

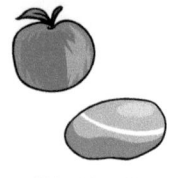

edible / inedible

hala pe / na hala pe

evil / kind

džungalo / šukar

excited / bored

bare vogjea / bi vogjea

fat / thin

thulo / kišlo

first / last

avgo / paluno

friend / enemy

amal / dušmani

full / empty

pherdo / čučo

hard / soft

zoralo / kovlo

heavy / light

pharo / lokho

hunger / thirst

bokh / truš

ill / healthy

nasvalo / sasto

illegal / legal

ilegalno / legalno

intelligent / stupid

godyaver / bigodyako

left / right

bajan / dahin

near / far

paše / dur

opposites - mamujipena

new / used

nevo / purano

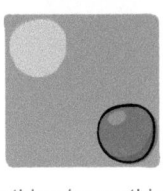

nothing / something

khanči / vareso

old / young

phuro / terno

on / off

phabardo / ačhavdo

open / closed

puterdo / phanlo

quiet / loud

mudro / bare avazeskoro

rich / poor

barvalo / čorolo

right / wrong

čačutno / došalo

rough / smooth

zoralo / kovlo

sad / happy

mazuni / lošalo

short / long

skurto / lungo

slow / fast

pohari / sigate

wet / dry

sapano / šuko

warm / cool

tato / šudro

war / peace

mareba / sansari

0

zero

zero

1

one

jek

2

two

duj

3

three

trin

4

four

štar

5

five

panč

6

six

šov

7

seven

efta

8

eight

ohto

9

nine

enja

10

ten

deš

11

eleven

dešujek

12
twelve
dešuduj

13
thirteen
dešutrin

14
fourteen
dešuštar

15
fifteen
dešupanč

16
sixteen
dešušov

17
seventeen
dešefta

18
eighteen
dešohto

19
nineteen
dešenja

20
twenty
biš

100
hundred
šel

1.000
thousand
milja

1.000.000
million
milioni

English
Anglicko

American English
Americko Anglicko

Chinese Mandarin
Kinesko Mandarinsko

Hindi
Indisko

Spanish
Špansko

French
Francusko

Arabic
Arapsko

Russian
Rusko

Portuguese
Portugalsko

Bengali
Bengalsko

German
Nemicko

Japanese
Japansko

I

thaj

you

tu

he / she / it

ov / oj

we

amen

you

tumen

they

ola

who?

ko?

what?

so?

how?

sar?

where?

kote?

when?

kana?

name

anav

behind

palal

in

andre

in front of

anglal o

over

upral

on

an

under

telal

beside

trujal

between

maškaral

place

than